THAT'S

a new collection

A

of utterly useless

FACT

information

JACK!

HARRY BRIGHT AND JAKOB ANSER

MJF BOOKS
new york

Published by MJF Books
Fine Communications
322 Eighth Avenue
New York, NY 10001

That's a Fact, Jack!
Library of Congress Number 2006929143
ISBN-13: 978-1-56731-810-4
ISBN-10: 1-56731-810-X

DESIGNED BY LISA CHOVNICK

Printed in the United States of America.

MJF Books and the MJF colophon are trademarks of
Fine Creative Media, Inc.

MV 10   9   8   7   6   5   4   3

THAT'S A
FACT, JACK!

DOLLY the sheep—the first cloned mammal—was named after country singer Dolly Parton. Stockmen dubbed the sheep "Dolly" because she was cloned from a mammary cell.

GREGOR Mendel, "the father of genetics," twice failed the certification exam to become a high-school science teacher.

POTATOES have more chromosomes than humans do—48 versus 46.

THE potato chip was created out of spite. In 1853, when a customer at Moon's Lake House in Saratoga Springs, New York, complained that head chef George Crum's potatoes were soggy and not salty enough, Crum stomped back to the kitchen, thinly sliced some potatoes, fried them until they were golden, poured salt all over them, and dumped them in front of the picky customer. They became known as "Saratoga chips" until Herman Lay, an enterprising young salesman, popularized the product throughout the country.

M R. Potato Head was the first
toy advertised on television.

UNLIKE other fruits, cranberries do not show their ripeness with color. Instead, they are sorted by bouncing. good cranberries bounce and bad ones don't.

THE steam rising from a cup of coffee contains the same amount of antioxidants as three oranges.

TOO much coffee can kill you. A lethal dose of caffeine for the average adult is somewhere around 10 grams, or the equivalent of drinking between 50 and 200 cups of coffee in rapid succession.

CAPHE CUT CHON (Vietnamese "fox dung coffee") is made from beans that have passed through the digestive system of a civet cat. With its long, sensitive snout, this finicky eater sniffs out the ripest coffee beans. Only the hardiest beans survive the digestive process intact and, according to aficionados, when brewed exhibit notes of wine, blueberries, caramel, and chocolate.

IVET, a honey-like secretion from a civet cat's genitals, gives off an unpleasant fecal odor, but in the right proportion transforms perfume into an aphrodisiac. Civet helped create the allure of the original Chanel No. 5.

I N 2005, the *New York Times* carried the headline "Good Smell Perplexes New Yorkers." The reported phenomenon was a mysterious maple-syrup scent wafting over the city. The smell's source was never identified.

ALTHOUGH the word "ghetto" today connotes impoverished urban centers, it originally pertained to quarters where Jews were forced to live, irrespective of social class. In Venice in the early 1500s, Jews were housed on an island with an iron foundry. The Italian word for foundry is *ghèto*.

PRETZELS originated in Northern Italy around A.D. 610. An Italian monk gave them out to children who had learned their prayers. He called the strips of baked dough, folded to resemble arms crossing the breast, *prestiolae* — Latin for "little rewards."

THE world's oldest surviving recipe is a formula for making beer. It was discovered outside Baghdad in 1850 on a 3,800-year-old Sumerian clay tablet. Two other tablets contain what are believed to be drinking songs.

CLEAVAGE has nothing to do with breast size or shape. Women with concave ribcages exhibit cleavage, while those with convex ribcages don't.

THE largest human cell is the female ovum. The smallest is the male sperm.

DROSOPHILA BIFURCA, a species of fruit fly, produces sperm that is nearly 6 centimeters long when fully uncoiled. That's roughly 1,000 times longer than human sperm and 20 times longer than the fruit fly itself.

THERE are roughly 144,000 mosquitoes for every person on earth.

MALARIA mosquitoes are attracted to ripe Limburger cheese and smelly feet. The odor-protein given off by the cheese was found to be structurally similar to human sweat.

MOSQUITO repellent doesn't repel mosquitoes; it blocks their sensors so that they don't know you are there.

A fetus acquires fingerprints by the end of the first trimester.

EVERY 20 minutes, the world's human population increases by 3,500. In the same time, one or more species of animal or plant life is wiped out—roughly 27,000 species per year.

B OOKWORMS are actually beetles. They proliferate in libraries, where dust, dirt, heat, darkness, and poor ventilation are prevalent. The mature female lays her eggs on the edges of books or in the crevices of bookshelves, and when hatched the larvae burrow into the books.

DR. Seuss wrote *Green Eggs and Ham* after his editor challenged him to produce a book using fewer than 50 different words.

THE first chapter of Joseph Heller's landmark *Catch-22* was published in the quarterly literary magazine *New World Writing* #7 in 1955 under the title "Catch-18." The same issue carried a chapter from Jack Kerouac's *On the Road*, published under a pseudonym.

IN 2003, the personal fortune of J. K. Rowling — best-selling British author of the wildly popular Harry Potter books — surpassed that of the Queen of England.

WINSTON Churchill had a heart attack in the White House while straining to open a bedroom window.

MEMBERS of the U.S. Congress are the world's highest paid legislators.

WILLIAM McKinley was the first president to ride in an electric car—the ambulance that took him to the hospital after he was shot by an assassin.

PRESIDENT Lyndon B. Johnson enjoyed Fresca so much that he had a special soda-pop tap installed in the White House.

A soda since 1884, Moxie is the only trademark to become an English word with a meaning beyond its product. "Moxie" is synonymous with pep, courage, and pluck.

ULCERS are not caused by spicy foods or stress. *Helicobacter pylori,* a spiral-shaped bacterium that thrives in the stomach's acid environment, causes nearly all peptic ulcers.

THE bristled toothbrush originated in China around the year 1498. The bristles, fixed to a bamboo or bone handle, were neck hairs from Siberian boars.

TOILET paper was invented by the Chinese. In 1391, the Bureau of Imperial Supplies began producing 720,000 sheets of toilet paper a year for exclusive use by the emperor. Each sheet measured 2 feet by 3 feet.

CHINESE recreational innovations: chess, fireworks, fishing pole and hook, hot air balloon, kite, and parachute.

THE ideal knuckleball should complete less than a single rotation on its way to home plate. Its erratic path is created by the difference in air molecules traveling over the baseball's seams and smooth surfaces.

ICE skaters skate on water, not ice. At 32° Fahrenheit, ice has a liquid surface measuring 40 billionths of a meter thick. Below 31° Fahrenheit, the liquid layer becomes so thin that a skater's blades would stick rather than glide across the ice.

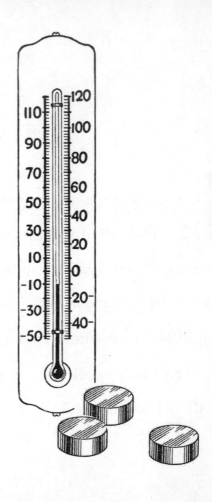

THE average lifespan of an NHL hockey puck is 7 minutes. Those that don't fly into the stands are removed because they warm up from friction and bounce on the ice. Game pucks—chilled to -10° Fahrenheit for maximum performance—are kept in a freezer in the penalty box.

"FORE!," the warning yelled by weekend duffers after hitting an errant golf shot, was originally an English military term. Back when soldiers fired rifles in lines, the command "Beware before!" was a signal for the front line to kneel or risk getting their heads blown off.

THE Spanish exclamation *Ole!*, commonly heard at bullfights and flamenco dances, comes from *Allah*, meaning "praise be to God."

A SSASSIN" comes from the Arabic word *hashshash*, meaning "one who smokes or chews hashish." During the Crusades, an arcane Muslim order called the Assassins terrorized invading Christians by carrying out secret murders while under the influence of hashish.

THE two robbers crucified next to Jesus were Dismas and Gestas. Their names are not mentioned in the Gospels but can be found in the Gospel of Nicodemus (Acts of Pilate), one of the many books of Christian Apocrypha.

IN 2006, the Gospel of Judas surfaced after 1,700 years. In it, Jesus asks Judas as his closest friend to give him over to authorities, telling Judas he will "exceed" the other disciples by doing so.

VOLTAIRE, the French philosopher, novelist, and ardent atheist, once held up the Bible and proclaimed, "In 100 years this book will be forgotten, eliminated." Less than 50 years after Voltaire's death, the Geneva Bible Society bought the house he grew up in—in order to produce and distribute Bibles.

ACCORDING to *Guinness World Records*, the Bible is the best-selling book of all time, with roughly 2.5 billion copies in distribution since 1815 in over 2,200 languages and dialects.

N 2004, the glossy Ikea catalogue overtook the Bible as the world's most distributed publication — 145 million copies versus 25 million copies.

THE Bible is the most shoplifted book in the world.

———————

ONE of the holiest Christian holidays is named after a pagan goddess. The word "Easter" derives from the Anglo-Saxon goddess Eostre, who governed the vernal equinox.

I N 1659, the Massachusetts General Court ordered a 5-shilling fine to be paid by anyone caught celebrating Christmas. The ban was revoked in 1681. Christmas did not become an official federal holiday until 1870, under President Ulysses S. Grant. New Year's Day, Independence Day, and Thanksgiving were all made federal holidays as part of the same legislation.

ACCORDING to a 2005 survey by CareerBuilder.com, 43% of Americans called in sick when there was nothing wrong with them, up from 35% the year before.

DISNEY World in Orlando, Florida, covers 30,500 acres (46 square miles). That's twice the size of Manhattan.

EACH year, when the Ringling Bros. and Barnum & Bailey circus comes to New York City, the last stage of the journey is made on foot. Spectators gather as a procession of adorned elephants is led through the Lincoln Tunnel—an event depicted in the film *Eternal Sunshine of the Spotless Mind*.

THROUGHOUT its lifetime, an elephant goes through six sets of teeth. The elephant starves to death once the sixth set of teeth falls out.

Butterflies are cannibals.

Tigers have striped skin under their hair but zebras don't.

CROCODILES do in fact produce tears. They have lacrimal glands, just like humans.

MONKEYS don't have feet.
Since they have opposable
thumbs instead of big toes, they are
classified as being four-handed.

UNDER the Federal Food, Drug, and Cosmetic Act, leeches and maggots are categorized as medical devices.

THE emerald cockroach wasp (*Ampulex compressa*) commandeers a cockroach in order to lay its egg inside the roach's exoskeleton. After delivering precise stings to paralyze the roach, the wasp—too small to carry its victim to a burrow—leads it by its antenna like a dog on a leash.

A COCKROACH'S brain is spread throughout its body. If you chop off its head, it can still live for up to a week. It finally dies because it can't eat.

THE South American paradoxical frog (*Pseudis paradoxa*) is so called because it gets smaller as it develops. It starts out as a 10-inch tadpole and "grows up" to become a frog about 3 inches long.

AN ant will often climb to the top of a grass stalk and seemingly wait there, becoming easy prey for roaming herbivores. Does this benefit the ant, or is it just a fluke? It is a fluke: the lancet liver fluke (*Dicrocoelium dendriticum*). Once inside the ant, the parasite controls its nerve centers, forces it into the open, and eventually finds safe harbor in the livers of sheep, cattle, goats, pigs, and, rarely, humans.

YOU can in fact get cooties.
Cooties are lice.

ALL scorpions glow.
A scorpion's exoskeleton contains a thin transparent film called the hyaline layer, which fluoresces under black (ultraviolet) light. Even after hundreds of millions of years, the hyaline layers of fossilized scorpions still glow.

POISON ivy is a member of the tropical Cashew family, from which we get cashew and pistachio nuts.

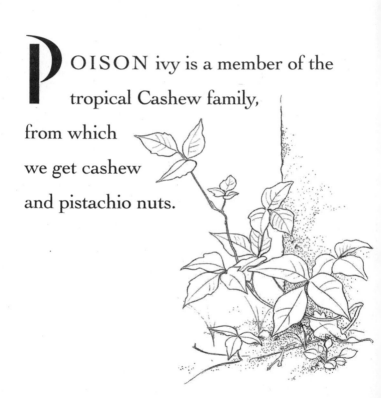

PROSOPAGNOSIA is the inability to recognize faces, including one's own image in a mirror. Sufferers of this rare disorder know that they are looking at a face but they cannot say to whom the face belongs.

CHARLIE Chaplin once lost a Charlie Chaplin look-alike contest. He failed even to make the finals.

GEORGE Clooney vowed never to remarry or have children, but Michelle Pfeiffer and Nicole Kidman each bet $10,000 that he'd be a father by age 40. On Clooney's fortieth birthday (May 6, 2001), the actresses conceded defeat and each sent a check. Clooney returned the money, betting double or nothing that he wouldn't have kids before turning 50.

ARTISTS have more sexual partners. Researchers suggest that creative people excel at attracting mates, acting on sexual impulses, and doing more than their share of ensuring species survival because they often display "schizotypal" characteristics — the positive side of schizophrenic personality traits.

IN his role as James Bond, Sean Connery wore a toupee to hide his receding hairline.

THE actress Liz Sheridan, best known for her portrayal of Jerry Seinfeld's TV mother, was briefly engaged to James Dean.

WHEN not sleeping, shrews must hunt constantly. After only a few hours without food, they become so weak that they begin to eat themselves.

F you are locked in a sealed room, you will die of carbon dioxide poisoning before your brain starves from oxygen deprivation.

THERE are rivers in the sky. Although they can't be seen with the naked eye, "atmospheric rivers" hundreds of miles wide cut enormous channels through the sky and play a key role in the planet's water cycle.

CLOUDS are made of water droplets condensed around particles of smoke, dust, ash, and salt.

CIGARS are called "stogies" because pioneer drivers of Conestoga covered wagons made in Lancaster, Pennsylvania, preferred the long, cheap cigars available in that region. Over time, "Conestoga" was shortened to "stogie."

THE word "curfew" comes from the French *couvre feu,* or "cover the fire." A curfew was originally the time when you had to extinguish fires, candles, and lamps.

IN late-1600s Puritan society, a child over 16 convicted of cursing at a parent was sentenced to death. Being a stubborn or rebellious child also earned you a death sentence.

THE Puritans brought beer to America. According to *Mourt's Relation* (1622), the *Mayflower* pilgrims settled at Plymouth because supplies, especially beer, were running low. Beer was a dietary mainstay on long voyages because, having been boiled, it was purer than water.

THE Puritans founded America's first college, bookstore, and newspaper.

WHAT in tarnation!" derives from the expression "What in eternal damnation!"

THE infinity sign is called a "lemniscate."

DESPITE being made famous by Dutch paintings and Spain's *Don Quixote*, windmills originated in Persia before the tenth century.

WEDDING rings date back thousands of years. The ancient Romans and Egyptians both believed that a vein called the *vena amoris* ran directly from the ring finger to the heart.

PERCENTAGE of American men who say they would marry the same woman if they had to do it all over again: 80%. Percentage of American women who say the same: 50%.

THE German language has words to describe 30 kinds of kisses, including *nachküssen*, which are kisses that make up for those that have been omitted.

ON average, women utter 7,000 words a day; men manage just over 2,000.

E T A O I N S H R D
L U C M F G Y P W B V K
X J Q Z :   the alphabet in order
of its frequency of use in written
English.

A "snowclone" is a familiar, oft-repeated phrase containing parts which can be substituted for comic, journalistic, provocative, or literary purposes. For example, the writers of *The Simpsons* took the phrase "Worst. Episode. Ever." from a *TV Guide* review and reappropriated it numerous times for their Comic Book Guy character, who says things like "Worst. Cross-over. Ever."

AT -90° Fahrenheit, your breath will freeze in midair and fall to the ground.

———————

ANTARCTICA is the only continent with no owls.

AT 840,000 square miles, Greenland is the world's largest island. It is three times the size of Texas.

THERE are 2,598,960 possible hands in Texas Hold 'Em.

A ten-gallon hat only holds about three-quarters of a gallon of liquid. It got its name from the Spanish word *galón*, which means "braid." Some Mexican cowboys, or *vaqueros*, wore as many as ten braided bands on their sombreros.

MAJOR Henry Wirtz was the only soldier convicted of war crimes during the American Civil War. Wirtz was the commanding officer of the Confederate prison in Andersonville, Georgia. Of the 49,485 prisoners who entered the camp, nearly 13,000 died from disease and malnutrition.

THE word "deadline" originated in Civil War prisons, where lines were drawn that prisoners passed only at the risk of being shot.

THE term "the whole nine yards" dates from World War II. When fighter pilots armed their planes, the .50 caliber machine-gun ammunition belts loaded into the fuselage measured exactly 27 feet. If a pilot fired all his ammo at one target, it got "the whole nine yards."

THE "D" in D-Day doesn't stand for anything. In military terms, D-Day and H-Hour are sometimes used for the day and hour on which a combat operation is to be initiated.

ALASKA contains both the westernmost and easternmost points in America: Amatignak Island (179°15'W) and Semisopochnoi Island (179°6'E), respectively.

THE largest American city in terms of area is Juneau, Alaska, at 3,255 square miles. Los Angeles ranks second at 498 square miles.

HAWAII is the only state in the United States that grows coffee.

CHEWING an apple is just as effective at waking you up in the morning as drinking a cup of coffee. The act of chewing works to stimulate the central nervous system.

THE oldest wad of chewing gum is 9,000 years old. Swedish researchers believe the birch resin was chewed and spat out by a Neolithic man looking to get high.

STANNOUS fluoride, the cavity fighter found in toothpaste, is made from recycled tin. Fluorides work in two ways: they reduce the ability of bacteria to make acids and they remineralize tooth areas that have been attacked by acids.

THERE are more living organisms on the skin of a single human being than there are human beings on the earth's entire surface. An average adult's skin has a surface area of 16 to 22 square feet, each square inch of which houses nearly 20 million microorganisms.

SKIN is the body's largest organ.
An average adult's skin weighs 8 to
10 pounds, making it two to three
times as heavy as the brain.

THE carat, standard unit of measurement for gemstones, was originally based on the weight of the carob seed.

A fundamental characteristic of nanotechnology is that nanodevices—structures at a size scale below 100 nanometers—self-assemble.

CITYWATCHER.COM, a video-surveillance data center in Ohio, was the first U.S. company to "tag" its workers as a way of identifying them. In 2006, the company planted RFID chips—inexpensive radio-frequency devices that transmit a unique identifying signal—in the right arms of two employees. In doing so, the company controlled access to security-video footage for government agencies.

ON March 15, 1985, Symbolic.com became the first registered Internet domain. Science-fiction writer William Gibson had coined the term "cyberspace" in his novel *Neuromancer* only the year before.

THE first item sold on eBay (then called AuctionWeb) was a broken laser pointer that sold for $14—at the time, more than the cost of a new one.

OVER 100 Barbie dolls are sold on eBay every hour.

ON February 8, 2000, the meaning of life was auctioned on eBay. The auction's description read: "I have discovered the reason for our existence and will be happy to share this information with the highest bidder." After eight bids were placed, the meaning of life was sold for $3.26.

AMERICAN inventor Thomas Edison held over 1,500 patents, including those for the phonograph, kinetoscope, dictaphone, radio, lightbulb, autographic printer, and tattoo gun.

THE first film version of *Frankenstein* was a 15-minute silent produced by Thomas Edison.

WHEN Thomas Edison died in 1941, Henry Ford captured his last breath in a bottle.

HENRY Ford invented the modern charcoal briquette from sawdust and scrap wood generated in his automobile factory. Ford encouraged people to use their cars on picnic outings by offering barbecue grills and Ford Charcoal at his automobile dealerships.

THE Tyrolean Iceman—the 5,300-year-old mummy of a Late Neolithic man found in 1991— was carrying a bark container with a charcoal ember in it.

HENRY Ford, Robert Fulton, Eli Whitney, and Paul Revere were all clockmakers at one point in their lives.

L EVI Hutchins made the first modern alarm clock in 1787. Fastidious by nature, Hutchins fashioned a mechanical ringing-bell clock so that he could arrive punctually at work each morning. He never bothered to patent or mass-produce his invention, which went off only at 4:00 A.M.

LEONARDO da Vinci invented and used an alarm clock in which water flowed in a thin stream from one receptacle to another. When the second receptacle was full, a system of gears and levers raised Leonardo's feet into the air.

GREEK mathematician and scientist Heron of Alexandria invented a water clock during Alexander the Great's reign. Its purpose was to limit the time a lawyer could speak in court.

INVENTIONS that changed how we shop: the cash register (1884), the shopping cart (1936), and the bar code (1952).

DESPITE the advent of technologies like Maytag washing machines, Dyson vacuums, and Proctor & Gamble Swiffers, the total time spent doing housework has remained constant since the 1920s: roughly 51 to 56 hours per week.

IN 2006 in America, women make 77 cents to every dollar men earn.

MEN who kiss their wives goodbye in the morning earn higher salaries than men who don't.

THE word "salary" comes from the Latin *salarium*, meaning "payment in salt." Roman soldiers were paid partially in salt, a highly valuable commodity at the time.

SINCE its establishment by Congress in 1913, the Federal Reserve has oversaw a 98% drop in the value of the U.S. dollar. In other words, today's dollar would have been worth 2 cents in 1913. Before the Fed's establishment, the purchasing power of the dollar remained constant for over a century.

WARREN Buffett, legendary investor and self-made multibillionaire, filed his first income tax return at age 13, reporting revenue from a newspaper delivery job. He claimed a $35 deduction for his bicycle.

THE word "economics" is derived from the Greek *oikos* ("house") and *nemein* ("manage").

THE influential banker J. P. Morgan once said that he would never lend money to a company in which the highest-paid employee was compensated more than 20 times the lowest-paid, as it was unstable in his view. Based on 2004 figures, the ratio of average CEO pay ($11.8 million) to worker pay ($27,460) was 431 to 1.

IF the minimum wage had risen as fast as CEO pay since 1990, the lowest-paid workers in the United States would have earned $23.03 an hour in 2005.

ACH floor of New York City's Twin Towers measured 208 feet by 208 feet—just 300 square feet shy of an acre. Each tower comprised 110 stories and corresponded to its own ZIP code.

THERE are more Subway
sandwich shops in Manhattan
than there are actual subway stations.

OVER the last 50 years, New York City taxi medallions — which are affixed to the hoods of official yellow cabs — have provided a 15% annual return to investors, far outperforming other investment classes. Over the same period, blue-chip stocks earned 8%, real estate 7%, and gold 6%.

IN 2005, a list ranked crime levels in 240 American cities with a population of 100,000 or more. Despite its reputation as a haven for criminals, New York City came in near the very bottom at 222nd.

THE term "cop" most likely derives from the British police acronym for Constable On Patrol. Some believe it is a shortened version of "copper," which referred to the buttons worn by British bobbies.

LONDON cab drivers have big brains. Acquiring exhaustive knowledge of London's labyrinthine roundabouts, mews, and one-ways actually causes portions of the drivers' brains to grow to larger-than-average sizes.

THE world's largest pancake was cooked in 1994 in England. It measured 15 meters in diameter, weighed 3 tons, and contained approximately 2 million calories.

THE custom of leaving undone the bottom button of a man's vest originated with King Edward VII of England, who reigned from 1901 to 1910. Bertie, as he was called, was simply too portly to fasten the bottom button. Taking it as a fashion statement, his loyal subjects followed his lead.

OLIVER Cromwell—the military leader who overthrew King Charles I of England and ruled as self-appointed Lord Protector from 1653 until his death in 1658—was posthumously hanged, and drawn and quartered in 1660 upon the Restoration of King Charles II.

JOHN Milton is believed to have used Cromwell as the basis for Satan in his epic poem *Paradise Lost*, published in 1667.

LUCIFER is Latin for "light-bringer."

ONE twenty-fifth of the energy released by an incandescent lightbulb is light. The rest is heat.

THE incredibly stable adhesive known as Super Glue was invented by accident in 1942 by Dr. Harry Coover. While trying to make optical coating materials, Coover would test their properties by placing them between two prisms and shining light through them. When he tried cyanoacrylate, he couldn't get the prisms apart.

HIGH-quality crystal produces a clear ringing sound when struck, hence the phrase "crystal clear."

_____

ICE is a mineral.

A "rusticle" is a rust formation similar to an icicle. It occurs under water when wrought iron rusts, as on shipwrecks.

ONE ton of iron will produce a ton and a half of rust.

B AMBOO is stronger than
concrete.

A 2-inch square of Velcro is strong
enough to hang a 175-pound
man from the ceiling.

VELCRO, barbed wire, and chain saws are all products designed to mimic natural structures: cockleburs, Osage orange thorns, and beetle grub teeth, respectively.

THE fly of your jeans is the fold of cloth over the zipper, not the zipper itself.

THE holes in wingtip shoes were originally introduced in Scotland and Ireland in the fourth century. These allowed water to drain from the shoes of locals as they negotiated their homelands' sodden terrain.

THE word "lap" comes from the French *lappet*, a jacket flap that hangs below the waist. Such garments were in vogue until the early twentieth century.

SHAKESPEARE coined thousands of new words, or "neologisms," in his plays and sonnets. Among these are: *amaze, bedroom, excellent, fitful, majestic, radiance,* and *summit.*

VEGETARIANISM is not a recent trend. Though John Cleese, Willem Dafoe, Bob Dylan, Samuel L. Jackson, B. B. King, Carl Lewis, Kate Moss, Muhammad Ali, Gwyneth Paltrow, Prince, and Jerry Seinfeld all practice vegetarianism, historical figures such as Apollonius of Tyana, Leonardo da Vinci, Thomas Edison, Albert Einstein, Mahatma Gandhi, Siddhartha Gautama (Buddha), Franz Kafka, Plato, Plutarch, Pythagoras, Mary and

Percy Bysshe Shelley, William Shakespeare, George Bernard Shaw, Isaac Bashevis Singer, Henry David Thoreau, Leo Tolstoy, H. G. Wells, and many others were vegetarians first.

25% of all the vegetables consumed in the United States are french fries.

———————

ONE out of five American meals is eaten in a car.

TWINKIES are 68% air and 32% Twinkie stuff, which means you can pack three Twinkies in the same space taken up by only one.

SADDAM Hussein's favorite American snacks are Raisin Bran and Doritos. He dislikes Froot Loops.

BUBBLE gum is pink because Walter Diemer, a Fleer employee, had only pink coloring left when he mixed up his first successful batch.

CHOP suey means "odds and ends" in Mandarin or "mixed bits" in Cantonese. It is a purely American dish and most likely dates back to the 1860s with early Chinese miners and railway workers.

WHILE filming a fight scene for *Enter the Dragon*, Bruce Lee performed a flying kick so fast it could not be seen at 24 frames per second. The cameraman re-filmed the sequence in slow motion so it would not appear faked.

N 2006, a Malaysian man received the largest phone bill in history. The bill—which the man contested—was roughly U.S. $218,000,000,000,000.

A Giant Mekong Catfish holds the record as the largest freshwater fish ever caught. Captured in Thailand on May 1, 2005, it weighed 646 pounds.

A calorie is the amount of energy, or heat, it takes to raise the temperature of one gram of water by one degree Celsius. A gallon of gasoline contains 31,000 kilocalories, or the equivalent of 46.3 Happy Meals.

YOU can tell the temperature by listening to a cricket chirp. For the temperature in degrees Fahrenheit, count the number of chirps in 15 seconds and then add 37.

THE ears of a cricket are located on its front legs, just below the knees.

SCIENTISTS at the Tokamak Fusion Test Reactor site in Princeton, New Jersey, have produced temperatures as high as 920 million degrees Fahrenheit, or about 34 times as hot as the center of the sun.

OF the four fundamental forces—gravity, electromagnetism, weak nuclear force, and strong nuclear force—gravity is by far the weakest.

THE surface of the light side of the moon is covered in tiny concave chips. Light hitting these chips from any direction is fully reflected outward. This same principle has been applied to the reflective paint used on road signs: the paint itself contains concave chips reminiscent of moondust.

IN 2006, the orbiting Cassini probe discovered liquid water on Saturn's moon, Enceladus, suggesting that conditions amenable to life may exist beyond earth but still within its solar system.

SATURN has such a low density that if placed in water it would float.

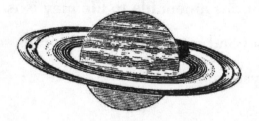

ABSOLUTE zero
(-459.67° Fahrenheit) is the
point at which all atomic motion
ceases. Outer space is the coldest
place in the universe, but it is three
degrees above absolute zero. Scientists
believe that heat left over from the
Big Bang keeps the temperature
from going any lower.

THE largest supply of alcohol in the universe is in deep space. Astronomers have spotted an alcohol cloud in the Milky Way that measures 288 billion miles across.

To see a rainbow you must have your back to the sun.

THE sudden, violent windstorms that rush up and down Mount Fuji contributed greatly to Japan's mythology, which includes many flying spirits.

SUMO wrestlers skip breakfast, then nap after lunch to gain and sustain their weight.

———————

HONCHO" comes from the Japanese word meaning "squad leader."

FRANCIS Ford Coppola made a Suntory whiskey commercial with legendary Japanese director Akira Kurosawa—an event depicted in Sofia Coppola's film *Lost in Translation*.

FOR the candlelit scenes in his eighteenth-century epic *Barry Lyndon* (1975), Stanley Kubrick invented his own camera. Using a lens borrowed from NASA, Kubrick built a camera whose shutter speed was beyond what is typical even today.

EDWARD Halley didn't just have a comet named after him. In 1693, the mathematician and astronomer wrote *An Estimate of the Degrees of the Mortality of Mankind*, which marked the beginning of actuarial science—the foundation of the modern life insurance industry.

MORPHINE was named after Morpheus, the Greek god of dreams.

———————————

LETTUCE contains two to ten parts of morphine per billion.

THE Bayer Company introduced heroin as a nonaddictive substitute for morphine in 1898. Ironically, morphine was eventually used to treat heroin addiction.

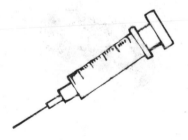

N the summer of 1967, Jimi Hendrix played seven gigs as the opening act for The Monkees.

NOT all bands are doomed to fail after losing their lead singer. After Joy Division's front man Ian Curtis died, the band reformed as New Order and released the best-selling 12-inch single of all time, "Blue Monday."

THE phrase "I laughed all the way to the bank" comes from the famously ostentatious Liberace. The pianist responded with this quip when a critic panned the kitschiness of his act.

HUMAN foreskins discarded after circumcision are sold to biomedical companies for use in artificial skin manufacture. One foreskin contains enough genetic material to grow 250,000 square feet of new skin. They are also used as a "secret" ingredient in popular antiwrinkle gels.

F you are gripped by panic because you think that someone has stolen your penis or that your penis is retracting into your body and disappearing, you are suffering from a rare psychological disorder called *koro*, or genital retraction syndrome (GRS). Minor *koro* epidemics have occurred for thousands of years in Asia.

CHRISTOPHER Columbus believed until he died that he'd landed in Asia instead of in the "new world."

THE Sargasso Sea in the North Atlantic—named after the sea-weed *sargassum* which floats over its expanse—is the saltiest part of all the world's oceans. The legend of the Sargasso Sea as the "sea of lost ships" predates the Bermuda Triangle's reputation by centuries.

I N 2006, paleontologists discovered a new species of meat-eating dinosaur larger than the *Tyrannosaurus rex*. Roaming in packs, the *Mapusaurus roseae* hunted even the largest known dinosaur, *Argentinosaurus*, which was 25% longer than the blue whale.

THE tongue of a blue whale weighs about as much as a full-grown elephant or a 2005 Hummer H2 Sport Utility Vehicle.

EVERY year, Arctic terns make the 25,000-mile round-trip between their breeding grounds in the Arctic circle and their wintering grounds in the Antarctic. They almost never land, and because of migration patterns they see more daylight than any other creature on the planet.

A falling object travels slower at the equator than it does at the North and South Poles.

_____

JELLYFISH are 95% water.

THE Great Barrier Reef is often referred to as the world's largest organism, but like all coral formations it is actually made up of many millions of tiny organisms.

A fungus known as the honey mushroom (*Armillaria ostoyae*) in the Malheur National Forest in eastern Oregon is the single largest organism on earth. Roughly 2,400 years old, it stretches 3.5 miles across and covers an area larger than 1,600 football fields—most of it hidden underground.